Signs

By Nick Rebman

SPARKS

Picture Glossary

bike sign 11

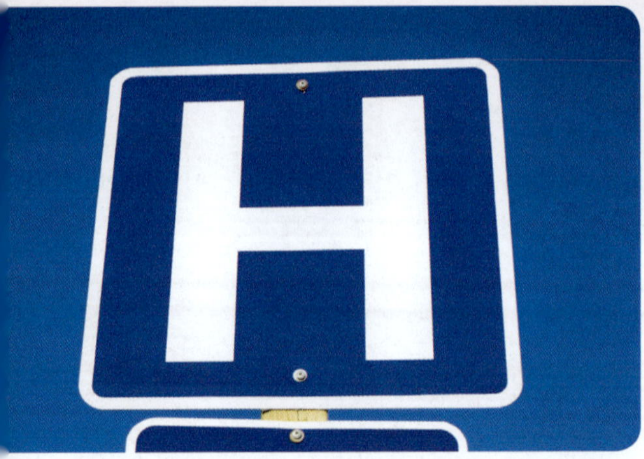

hospital sign 13

STOP

RAIL ROAD
CROSSING

I see signs.

Signs keep us safe.

signs

I see signs.

This sign tells us to stop.

stop sign

I see signs.

This sign tells us how fast we can go.

speed sign

I see signs.

This sign is for a bike.

Bikes can go here.

bike sign

This sign is for a hospital.

A hospital is near.

hospital sign

This sign is for a train.

The train tracks are near.

train sign

Do You Know?

What sign do you see?

stop sign

hospital sign

bike sign

train sign